AUTOBIOGRAPHY OF CLAY

poems by

Anita N. Feng

Finishing Line Press
Georgetown, Kentucky

AUTOBIOGRAPHY
OF CLAY

*This books is dedicated to all those who have touched clay
and fallen in love*

ACKNOWLEDGMENTS

"What To Do with a Rongo Jar" in *ADANNA*
"The First Golem" and "The Grandmother of Clay Might Grow Angry" in *TIFERET*
"How Red Was Discovered" in *LEAPING CLEAR*

Publisher: Leah Huete de Maines
Editor: Christen Kincaid
Cover Art and Design: Katrina Noble
Author Photo: Katrina Noble

Order online: www.finishinglinepress.com
also available on amazon.com

Author inquiries and mail orders:
Finishing Line Press
PO Box 1626
Georgetown, Kentucky 40324
USA

Contents

Beloved, we walk on the fragile edge
Of a heap of earth...

—from "Pilgrimage," by Cesar Vallejo, translated by James Wright

THE GRANDMOTHER OF CLAY

For billions of years I've been grinding my teeth in my sleep,
shattering mountains in my jaws, my arms and shoulders locked
over this hoard of flinty clay.

But the real reason I don't sleep at night is because I'm on guard
against the wind, rivers, and rain that steal my clay away.

So when some bright-eyed, ignorant child saunters by with the
aim to just take some, you can be sure I'll let her know the price.

Every time her precious pots crack or fall apart, her problems will
be the same as mine.

She should know better. She should be more reckless and divine.
And she should leave something of use behind.

GENESIS OF HUNGER

If the origin of life wasn't a roll of the dice or an *abracadabra* of
the divine, then surely it began with volcanic clay as it rested in
stagnant pools, viscous and benign. Clay has always been like
that, the modest incubator for all the whims of space and time.

Eons ago this blue-gray clay known as bentonite became a
wayside inn for evolutionary debris, where floating strands of
RNA met and experimentally combined.

For millions of years, clay played host to countless accidental
pairings and rendezvous, welcoming all comers—precocious
proteins, addled memories, along with the celestial garbage that
would evolve into our very own DNA.

Until eventually, we crawled out of the mud-soaked water with
legs and a tail and a terrific hunger to stay alive.

THE FIRST GOLEMS

As it is written by the hand of mystery, we were gathered
from all the clay on earth in a formless, amorphous
beginning. Nevertheless we grew, establishing extremities of
foolish courage, a common torso of appetites and a strong
spinal column built of stubborn self-regard.

We dried, and as cracks appeared, we split in two, right down
the middle.

Fired by sunlight, we shrank, making room for each other
and all the progeny that followed. We called each other by
self-made names.

Someday our bodies will crumble to clay dust again. So be
it. We'll gather what's left and make it over into whatever
adamandeve wonder comes next.

FISH

How can we know in advance when that pivotal event will occur,
or what form it will take?

One day, when I was young, I looked up and saw a handmade
clay fish hanging on a friend's kitchen wall and that was that; I
was thrown into a sudden ocean of grace.

The satin-glazed fins cast the slant of afternoon sun into diamond
and cobalt blues.

The ceramic mouth opened wide for all the silica, feldspars, and
ash that had taken the place of water. I felt the living gasp.

Like one who falls in love, like one who's been baptized by bold
invention, the fish's wadded eyes opened my own to a theology
made entirely of clay.

ONE THOUGHT POLE-VAULTS INTO ANOTHER

Maybe I could make a living out of clay. Maybe wander across the country as an itinerant peddler of mud-made merchandise.

More taken with poetic phrasing than practicality, little credit was given to the fact that I knew nothing of clay and had no grasp on the mechanics of craft or money. No matter! I'd take an introductory class in learning how to throw.

After that, I'd live in the country and marry the shy boat captain that I'd met just the week before. The handmade life formed easily in my mind.

Winters would be for making wondrous artifacts out of clay, summers for sailing and fishing, and all year round we'd live off the proceeds forevermore.

HOW TO MAKE A GOOD MISTAKE[1]

There was no light anywhere and the animal people stumbled
through darkness until they finally realized that a little
illumination would help.

Grandmother Spider volunteered to fetch some. As she explained,
she was insignificant and small, so if things went wrong it
wouldn't be a great loss.

With her many delicate hands, she gathered up the clay. Slowly,
slowly, she coiled a little bowl that she would use to carry a piece
of sunlight home. She walked backwards as she worked, around
and around.

Then off she went eastward, spinning a thread behind her so she'd
find her way back.

Or so she thought.

But she'd grown dizzy from her labors, and instead of walking
in a straight line, she walked in circles, creating a beautifully
patterned web.

And as she spun her web going nowhere, the light came,
generously, to meet her right where she was.

CLAY SCHOOL

The new devotees enter the darkened sanctuary from which
we vow to emerge as potter creators. We scan the room with
barely contained terror. What will become of us?

Clay presides everywhere—stacked in bags or practiced in
ornate chaos over workbenches, slop buckets, embryonic
pots, all the while smeared on eyeglasses, overalls, and errant
strands of hair.

The grimed-over factory windows allow for just enough
obscure light for our hands to learn the liturgy of craft. We
listen to the plainsong of clay slapped against clay.

We watch with just enough courage to imagine the objects
we might yet make. If not today, then tomorrow. If not a
thing of beauty, at least a slag heap of flawed beginnings and
a sober reckoning of dreams.

HISTORY LESSON

After the earth was gathered up from intergalactic waste, molten matter hardened into basalt. Crystals and minerals grew into monumental wonders.

Then the grand erosions began (onslaughts of water, eruptions, hard and withering fractures). Surface rock broke apart and crumbled by infinitesimal degrees over the course of eons.

As all things faulted and decomposed, an elegant formula materialized: stone plus time equals clay. Artistry followed. Quartz and feldspars mixed with ash. The presence of iron evoked a reddish brown. Mica contributed a flash of light.

The already ancient clay then lay at rest in deltas and river beds, awaiting creation as only novice gods can do, in abundance and natural joy.

I AM KHNUM[2]

I materialize as the potter God of the inundation silt.

Because of me, the Nile floods, and because of me the fields are
nourished.

Master of creation, I have made myself.

I shape and guide each sentient being to their birth and organic
form. My arms surround you. I steady your fragile thoughts and
safeguard your limbs as I raise you up.

I created the Pharaoh's mother on my potter's wheel. I form birds
from the sweat of my body and fish from the pools in which I
bathe.

All that I have made is alive and abiding. All that I have made is
who you are today.

CENTERING INSTRUCTIONS FOR THE POTTER'S WHEEL

Slam the clay on the wheel head.

Turn the wheel up to top speed and give over every atom of faith to the centrifugal force that will bring this unruly mass to center.

Breathe, even as the fear between your cupped hands starts up a trembling insurrection, even as the clay refuses to reconcile to your ideas.

Then guide the material (and the maker) inward.

Anchor your elbows on your thighs. Steady the pulse of your misgivings.

Mud will splatter. Collateral damage will be displayed in full. Even if half the clay falls away, center what's left. Find your way to stillness at the very eye of your self-made storm.

THE ART OF CRAFT

While craftsmanship might describe the work, it hardly dignifies
the artistry of what we do as our role shifts from master to
mortician, salesman to slave, to indentured faith-keeper.

One incarnation believes in income and another, imagination.
Most of the time we are just the repair technician tackling
damage control with all hands flying, furiously engaged. We work
through the night with accidental beauty up our sleeves, and
sometimes, with invention sparkling at our fingertips.

THE CRAFT OF ART

Once upon a time, craft was art and art was craft and all of us
made our own hand-forged wings.

Imperfect labor dovetailed with invention. Weaving a shawl
provided better insight than words. And erratic wonder eroded
the worst of our dread with bits of wood or ink or thread.

Even now, we might come in out of the industrial cold to create
something like a bowl that holds everything as true.

WEDGE

This is how it works: when a potter and a boat captain are thrown together in holy matrimony,

everything gets wedged into a headwind of bewildering despair. Raw clay doesn't float. Salt water ruins glazes.

All our good intentions (slammed together, stacked up high and near to keeling over) are cut back down to size.

Clay gets thrown against reefed sails. Promises hang over the edge.

His liquor spills into my mud-stained heart. Impossible to shape or hold.

KNEAD

Shouldn't love be like kneading clay, rhythmic as blending and folding into one another? Like taking the bulk of a brief life and lifting from way back, turning present over past, bending false into true, the ragged into the smooth—shouldn't marriage be like that?

Shouldn't this be how beginnings lead to momentum with the heel of one hand bearing down to the clay's center, with desire on repeat and difficulties dispersed in a steady counter-clockwise motion—hand, arm, head and shoulder, leaning in?

Shouldn't this be where misgivings give way to method, where clay becomes willing and every misunderstanding steers us into the one, harmonious future we'd planned?

REMEDIAL THROWING LESSONS

Once fixed to the wheel-head, rudimentary forms stagger and
sway.

Notions of symmetry buckle under pressure while air bubbles
sabotage the walls. One after another, shapes collapse, weakened
by overwork and too much water.

So this is where the dream goes—enthusiasm tempered by
failure, failure tempered by gains that are so small as to be almost
indistinguishable from loss. All this followed by half a heart's
worth of effort ending with poor results.

And yet, by some strange maneuverings of subterranean hope,
a stubborn hunger still lives in my hands. Circling back to the
studio I call out to my clay, *I'm coming*, to try again.

NOTE TO SELF

Forget the old excuses and self-sabotaging ploys of giving up.
Better to tear into a good mistake and call it unmistakable.

Better to remake yourself from scratch if necessary, and leap
between moveable, dissolving goals because there is always
another way to live.

Remember the mud pies you made and wallowed in as child.

Liberate disappointment from the record books. And dare to
allow for something new to happen next.

WHAT TO DO WITH A RONGO JAR³

Once upon a time, back when the earth was soft and aching, a girl was born onto a ratty shawl in the rainy season. Her mother named the infant Ahjide, which means "born during a rainstorm", and then went about her business. No big deal.

Ahjide was born into poverty and later married into the lowest class, a family of potters, on her eleventh birthday. She was the only daughter of a mother who kept an untidy house, so she was the likeliest bride. No young woman would be crazy enough to want to be a potter. But that was the established rule. Men worked with hard materials like tin; women worked with clay. Everyone suffered.

This is what Ahjide learned about her trade:

The God Amma created humans directly from clay. New rongo jars are made for a marriage. A husband can insult his wife by breaking one of her pots. She, on the other hand, could cut off his rights of access by turning the rongo jar upside down.

Troubles, children, and pottery came and went. Finally, when she was fifty years old, the oldest living person in her village, maybe even in the whole of Africa, she set out for the forest of the dead with her dead husband's rongo jar. Night and morning had only just begun trading places. She sat beside a quiet pool to rest -- its placid surface, a mirror.

For the first years of their marriage her husband had paid no attention to her. He would go hunting or work at tin. Ahjide stayed behind with the other girls and played with them. She cooked yams in the rongo jar when he returned, and he would eat, making such annoying noises with his lips that she hated to look at him. But over time, they had gotten used to each other. Now it was the day after her husband's funeral and she needed to deliver his pot to the place in the forest where his spirit waited.

But his spirit could wait a little longer. The pond where Ahjide rested was rimmed with a yellow clay. Her hands started to poke around of their own accord, looking for a good vein. Old habits for old hands.

She scratched out a handful, moistened it with a little spit and worked the clay into a figure of a child. Then she said to her, "Though we potters are the despised class, I don't care anymore. When I was young I wished for another kind of life. But now the clay is who I am and I'm fine with that. Why? Because I make the end of my story into the beginning of yours."

WHAT COMES AFTER 10,000 BROKEN POTS

It's a fragile item, clay.

So we add grog to our brittle bones and bentonite to our bloodstream as we watch our pottery break apart, warp, slump, or shatter.

We fuel our resolve as one over-fired pot collapses, another explodes, and yet another melts, fused to the now ruined kiln shelf.

What a fine art it is—the letting go of the latest lost cause. But to go back down to the studio, down to the heart and soul mines against all odds…

that's how we turn 10,000 disasters into the one spark that ignites us all over again.

RECYCLING

Like the unfinished life, unfired clay can be reclaimed. There's no need to throw out all those brow-beaten and heavily misbegotten bowls. No need to hoard them either.

To start over, first remove any foreign objects (false pretenses, bits of hubris) that have managed to burrow within.

Dry the clay thoroughly, then add water. And before your eyes, everything will dissolve. You'll see that fatally flawed vase disintegrate into a heap. What could be more delightful? Like a mountain laid down to mud in a minute.

Soon the clay will dry enough to reshape. All is forgiven, if not forgotten. All is feasible, again.

ALCHEMY OF CHANCE

Fifty thousand years ago, a woman set a reed-woven basket lined
with clay too close to the fire. She had other things on her mind.
Fear, for example, and the constant threat of loss and desire. And
the problem of how to stay alive.

When she returned, hours later, the reeds in her basket had burnt
away. But left behind was a hardened clay bowl. What had once
been dull gray, was now reddish-brown, shimmering in the ashes.
Tapping the edge, it rang.

The possibility occurred to her that this kind of bowl might
be useful. It might even turn out to be something that lasts.

ALCHEMY OF CHOICE

Fifty thousand years ago, a child shaped a figure of her dead mother out of clay and threw it in the fire as a despondent way to say goodbye.

The next day the figure hadn't disappeared. It hadn't burned to ash like her mother's body. Instead, the effigy was still there, glimmering with a bright, reddish hue in the warm coals. Her mother-in-clay, now shrunk in size, was hardened to such a degree that it could be carried anywhere without falling apart.

This clay mother never cried and never died.

With reverence, the child spoke to her mother spirit, and the child, all by herself, soon started to come alive.

ALCHEMY OF CHANGE

Fifty thousand years later, a woman built a wood-fired kiln.
She wanted to create a glaze known as ox-blood red—a warm,
reddish color that required a reduction firing method, something
a state-of-the-art downdraft kiln could do.

She layered bricks as she considered her years layered with clay,

*The clay and I, we're set alight by passion. We've seen the patterns:
once the match is lit, all reasonable reservations evaporate.*

*Then comes vulnerability and transformation, the body exposed to
the furnace.*

*And finally, we arrive at irreversible change. Our bodies shrink and
vitrify, and harden into whatever unknown eternity happens to
come next.*

HOW TO REVERSE ENGINEER THE EVOLUTION OF OUR WORLD

It took a gazillion years for the earth's original molten mass to cool, break down, and disperse.

However, in a matter of hours, a kiln works that same magic backwards.

Clays are gathered and built up into forms, then fired to near molten heat—flames entangled with smoke and ash like so much stardust.

No wonder we humans pride ourselves on our ingenuity. No wonder we wreak such monumental havoc and invent as much beauty as we do.

HOW RED WAS DISCOVERED[4]

Long ago, in the antiquity of China, the tradition of pottery-
making was a communal affair.

In order to prepare the clay, the raw material had to be siphoned
from the earth by slaves and filtered in pools by peasants until the
clay had the color and refinement of ivory clouds.

Then the clay was set aside to be aged until it embodied the
aroma of fermented wisdom.

At that time, there lived a master potter by the name of Ah-Wei.

One day, when he was supervising the unloading of the great
dragon kiln, he felt forebodings. As always, his fire stokers had
tended the dragon's thirst, but things had gone wrong toward the
end. One of the new stokers had thrown in a piece of wood that
was much too big for that late stage of firing, and it choked off the
air flow.

Huge clouds of smoke rolled up to heaven and spoiled the sleep
of the deceased.

Ah-Wei was furious and ordered the fire pits closed. He refused
to speak to anyone, least of all his wife, and slept at the furthest
end of their cot. In fitful dreams, he mourned the losses that
would be forthcoming.

Once the kiln had cooled, Ah-Wei went out alone to unbrick the
opening of the first chamber. With the solemnity of practicing
funeral rites, he removed the bricks, one by one, tier after tier. But
when he saw the first pots, despair transformed to hope when he
saw how these glazed pots glistened with a depth that surpassed
the traditions of the grandfathers.

Then, on a far back corner shelf of the kiln, he noticed a vase that had a brilliant flash of red coursing over its shoulder like a wave. Ah-Wei nearly swooned with wonder. Glazes had always been limited to grays, greens, browns, and blues. No one had ever achieved such a result as this before.

With the red vase cradled in silk he carried it directly to the emperor and presented it as a special gift. The emperor was enchanted and commissioned his master potter to make more.

Time passed, but Ah-Wei could not duplicate his red pot. He tried all combinations of ores and oxides. He sent teams of potters to the farthest regions of China to find red in the earth but they brought back nothing better than their own blood.

Finally, after many months, the emperor grew impatient and demanded that red pots be presented to him within a week's time or the potter would be killed.

Ah-Wei had no option to experiment further. He had only enough time to load the kiln and to fire what wares were at hand.

During the last stages of what would be the last firing of his life, he sat on his heels on a flattened rock near the mouth of the kiln. Ah-Wei had changed. Since the firing of the red glaze, he had acquired a new son. And this son had, at the moment of his birth, filled him with such a reservoir of love, such a lost valley of feeling.

He recognized his insubstantiality, how gains and losses balance out in strange ways.

When the kiln was at near-white heat, he went up to the kiln's
peephole, and with long iron tongs, pulled out a test ring. He
looked carefully, but still, there was no red in the glaze, not even
a spot.
Ah-Wei, in a fit of despair, grabbed the stone he had been sitting
on and threw it into the fire pit. All was finished. He went home
to his wife and child, and held them both in his arms.

Days later, when the kiln had cooled down, no one could find
the master potter, so a few stokers decided to open the kiln
themselves. To their amazement, on the face of each pot flashed
the emperor's red glaze, like the rosy blush on a child's warm
cheek.

THE CRAFTSPEOPLE'S CHORUS

Setting out before dawn, we leave our suburbs and cities for the pop-up, state-of-the-art version of an old village fair.

Once arrived, our vans, trucks, U-Hauls and jury-rigged old cars vie for the spot nearest our booths. We unload stock and a jigsaw puzzle of shelving parts. And when our blood and guts are all neatly arranged on display, we're open for business and ready to make change.

From our high director's chairs, we survey opening day. Soon a clown appears, juggling time and space, a whistle, a handmade mask, or whatever else happens to comes to hand.

In the distance, a weaver unwraps a stack of shawls, colors unwinding like a magician's cloak of birds.

A blacksmith, sleeves rolled up to his shoulders, stretches his arms wide and gives a terrific yawn that just about swallow the fairgrounds whole. Then the show begins.

Customers ask if we have mark-downs for seconds.

"They're all seconds," we reply in a heartbeat.

"How long does it take to make one?"

"It's taken all our lives," we reply, "and deranged as it sounds, we're still trying to make one right."

WILD CLAY

After forty odd years as a potter, here I am, teetering with spade
and bucket and old age, to scavenge for raw clay. Hard to believe
it's taken so long for me to go out and dig my own. But here I
am, just beyond the No Trespassing sign, just before the stagnant
pond where I've been told there's a good vein.

I scan the ground, searching through tall grass, under flinty
outcrops of rock until there it is—a hoard of musty clay.

I know you.

Here we are. Squeezed between my arthritic fingers, the
primordial mix yawns. With hands hungry for form, I shape a
wad of clay into a little bowl. The clay responds with an almost
living motion as it settles into its own weight and contours.

I find myself moved—right down to my elemental wild core.

MY NAME IS AH

As my body ages in the golden wind, I practice extending the
realm of being alive into a more panoramic view.

All the artistry in the world will outlive these over-large hands.

As I breathe in earth, air, mist—I marvel at how we mirror one
other. What is the beginning or end of a mountain anyway? Of
love, or clay?

Inhaling questions before they form into words,

I exhale this life like a breeze blowing through clouds. The
borrowed breath, prophet of mysteries yet to come. Ah...

Endnotes

1 my version of an old Cherokee legend

2 my version of the Egyptian legend, https://en.wikipedia.org/
   wiki/Khnum

3 an original story based on African legends, source: *Smashing
   Pots: Works of Clay from Africa*, by Nigel Barley

4 an original story based on a Chinese legend of how reduction
   firing was discovered.

In one slim collection of prose poems, **Anita Feng** tells an intimate story of that extraordinary raw material, clay, starting from the beginning of the cosmos to what we can dig out of our own backyard. Blending science and mythology along with her life-long career in working with clay, Anita examines the question: what is clay really, and how should we behave together? How is it possible to make an original life out of unruly mud? And how much will it cost? As these questions imply, to understand clay is the same as understanding ourselves. From the poem, "Recycling", *Like the unfinished life, unfired clay can be reclaimed. There's no need to throw out all those brow-beaten and heavily misbegotten bowls. No need to hoard them either.*

www.ingramcontent.com/pod-product-compliance
Lightning Source LLC
Chambersburg PA
CBHW020223090426
42734CB00008B/1196